E
780
WAR

APR 1 2 2005

DISCARDED
PROPERTY OF
KENAI COMMUNITY LIBRARY

M is for Melody

A Music Alphabet

Written by Kathy-jo Wargin and Illustrated by Katherine Larson

Text Copyright © 2004 Kathy-jo Wargin
Illustration Copyright © 2004 Katherine Larson

All rights reserved. No part of this book may be reproduced in any manner
without the express written consent of the publisher, except in the case of brief
excerpts in critical reviews and articles. All inquiries should be addressed to:

Sleeping Bear Press
310 North Main Street, Suite 300
Chelsea, MI 48118
www.sleepingbearpress.com

© Thomson Gale, a part of the Thomson Corporation.
Thomson and Star Logo are trademarks and Gale and
Sleeping Bear Press are registered trademarks used
herein under license.

Printed and bound in Canada.

10 9 8 7 6 5 4 3 2 1

Library of Congress Cataloging-in-Publication Data

Wargin, Kathy-jo.
M is for melody : a music alphabet / written by Kathy-jo Wargin ;
illustrated by Katherine Larson.
p. cm.
ISBN 1-58536-215-8
1. Music—History and criticism—Juvenile literature. 2. English language—
Alphabet—Juvenile literature. [1. Music. 2. Alphabet.] I. Larson, Katherine, ill.
II. Title.
ML3928.W37 2004
780—dc22
[E]   2003026229

This book is dedicated to all children who hear music in their hearts and have the courage to let that music be heard whether it sounds perfect or not. And to my parents who drove me to Nashville for an audition when I was 18, and had to listen to me sing—nonstop and out of tune— all the way there…and back. Thank you.

KATHY-JO

♪

This book is dedicated to my mother who gave me the gift of music as a child and to Maestro Barrachi who helped me develop my passion into a career.

KATHERINE

A a

An anthem is a special song of praise or loyalty written to honor a person or place. Most countries in the world have their own anthem, and to each nation, it is a beloved song sung at special celebrations and events.

The anthem of the United States of America is "The Star Spangled Banner," the Canadian anthem is "O Canada," and Mexico's is "Himno Nacional Mexican," which means the "National Anthem of Mexico."

A is for Anthem
        and we are so proud.
It's our national song
        and we sing it out loud.

B is for Brass.
Do you hear the sound swell
as it flows through the tubing
and out through the bell?

With trombones and trumpets
that shimmer and shine,
cornets and tubas
and French horns are fine!

trumpet

trombon

french horn

Oom-Pah-Pah! Oom-Pah-Pah!

The brass family includes the trumpet, trombone, French horn, tuba, and cornet. The brass section typically sits behind the woodwind section in most bands, and has some of the loudest instruments. A brass instrument is played by blowing air through or making lip vibrations upon the mouthpiece and into the instrument. As the player presses down on the valves or moves a slide, a different pitch is made. Brass instruments have curved tubes and a bell shape at the end.

Although a saxophone is made of brass, it is not a member of the brass family. It is a woodwind.

B b

C is for Conductors,
waving in the air.
They direct the music
with a special flair.

And C is for Composer.
Have you heard of Bach?
A composer writes the music,
from classical to rock!

The conductor is responsible for helping a group of musicians, usually a band, orchestra, or choir, rehearse and perform. The conductor is the person in front who uses a baton to help the musicians establish the tempo and dynamics, and directs the musicians on when to start and when to stop playing.

A composer is a person who writes music. There are many different styles of music that you can write—classical, jazz, pop, country and western, blues, rock and roll, symphonic, and many more. There are many well-known composers—Wolfgang Amadeus Mozart was a famous classical composer, and so was Ludwig von Beethoven. Paul McCartney is a famous contemporary composer. Clara Schumann and Fanny Mendelssohn were famous women composers.

Now **D** is for the Drum majors.
Don't you think they're grand,
  as they march on down the street
as leaders of the band?

D is also for Dynamic,
    it tells you how to play.
"Piano" means to play it soft,
    for loud wc say "fortc" (for-tay).

forte = louder

piano = softer

forte
piano

Drum majors are responsible for leading the marching band. They set the tempo of the march and the music, and the band follows their leadership.

The word dynamic means volume. It is the level of soft or loud that we should play or sing. For instance, the word "piano" means softly, while "forte" means to play or sing loudly. You can find these words on sheet music, where they will tell you how to begin the piece, and instruct you if you need to change your dynamic during the piece. There are also dynamic symbols that look like this: $<$ $>$. They mean to increase or decrease your volume.

D d

E e

To most people, the term early music is used for European classical music, with the most familiar pieces written in the 1700s and 1800s. Early music includes three important periods: Medieval from about A.D. 500 to A.D. 1430; Renaissance, from the mid 1400s to 1600, which is characterized by smooth melodies and rich harmonies; and Baroque, which dates from approximately the 1600s to 1750. Baroque music sounds very full, and is dramatic.

Some of the instruments used to make early music were the harpsichord, lute, recorder, and harp. Have you ever heard the music of Johann Sebastian Bach or Antonio Vivaldi? If so, then you have heard early music.

Now E is for the Early music
very long ago.
Medieval, Renaissance, and Baroque
are three kinds you should know.
Bravo! Bravo!

A folk song is a traditional song that belongs to the common folk music of a people or region. A folk song is often passed from person to person or region to region, so it is difficult to know where it began. It is typically about work, life, or love. Folk songs are important because they reflect how people see the world. Most often they are easy to sing and to play.

There are many folk songs we all know, such as "Yankee Doodle," "Skip to My Lou," and "On Top of Old Smokey." "Alouette" is a famous folk song from Canada. Some countries share folk songs—there are both American and Canadian verses to "This Land is Your Land." Do you know any folk songs from other lands?

Ff

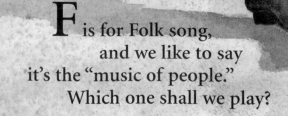

F is for Folk song,
and we like to say
it's the "music of people."
Which one shall we play?

The letter **G** is for Guitar,
you strum or play with picks.
Some guitars have twelve strings,
others just have six.

A guitar is a popular instrument in the United States. It is a flat-backed instrument with a long fretted neck, and usually has six or twelve strings that are played by plucking or strumming. There are many different types of guitars—electric, bass, acoustic, steel, and Hawaiian, to name a few.

The guitar as we know it today most likely originated in Spain as long ago as the early 1500s. Although it has gone through many changes, it still remains an important folk instrument in many countries.

H is for Harmony.
It sounds very fine
when two or more notes
are played at the same time.

Harmony is when you hear two or more different pitches or tones playing at the same time. Harmony is what makes a melody sound more interesting.

Have you ever heard a chord? A chord is when three or more different tones are played at the same time and they are usually used to accompany a melody line. Chords are read vertically, which means up and down, because the notes are "stacked" on top of each other.

And **I** is for Instrument.
    Which one will you play?
When you join the band,
    you'll have fun every day!
Practice makes perfect.

An instrument is anything used to make music. Instruments can be large and fancy, like a grand piano, or small and portable, like a harmonica.

Instruments are grouped into families. The brass family includes the trumpet, French horn, trombone, tuba, cornet, and baritone. Important members of the wood-wind family are the flute, piccolo, clarinet, bassoon, English horn, oboe, and saxophone. The strings include violins, violas, cellos, and basses. Familiar members of the percussion family include the bass drum, snare and timpani, marimbas, xylophone, and cymbals.

You can make your own instruments, too. Find interesting things in your home and see what types of sounds they make. This is how some of the first instruments were created.

Ii

J j

Now J is for Jazz—
it's a cool music style.
It's a blend of our cultures
and it makes us smile.

There's Dixie and blues.
There's big band and swing.
Jazz started it all
and that's why it's king.

Jazz is an important type of music in American history. When people from Africa were brought to America as slaves, they brought their music with them in the form of slave work songs and spirituals. In the 1800s, settlers from many places such as England, Scotland, and Germany came to live in New Orleans, a U.S. city that had been shaped by French and Spanish culture and was also home to many African Americans. As these immigrants started making music with African-American musicians, they blended their sounds to create what we know today as jazz. Because of that, New Orleans is often referred to as the birthplace of jazz.

Some of the great jazz musicians include Louis Armstrong, Miles Davis, Billie Holiday, Duke Ellington, and Benny Goodman.

Can you scat? Let's try, cool cat.
Yibby-dooby-skip-skip-ba-doo!

K is for Keyboard.
Do you see the keys?
When you play with your hands,
    you "tickle the ivories."

Pianos, organs, harpsichords,
synthesizers, too—
all are keyboards we can play.
    I will try, will you?

The keyboard family includes familiar instruments such as the piano and organ. It also includes some not-so-familiar instruments like the harpsichord and synthesizer. These keyboard instruments are highly versatile, because they can be used in many ways—to provide interesting parts to bands and orchestras, to play two at a time as in a duet, or as a brilliant solo instrument.

Long ago, most pianos had keys made out of ivory. Today, most are made out of synthetic materials. Can you play the piano? Learning to play the piano provides good musical knowledge for any future musician!

k
k
K

And L is for the Lullaby,
a lovely song for sleep.
Shall we go to bed, my dear?
Hush, don't make a peep!

A lullaby is a beautiful, soft-sounding piece of music that is meant to be sung or listened to at night, especially when trying to fall asleep. The song is meant to lull someone to sleep.

One of the most well-known lullabies is "Lullaby," written by Johannes Brahms. Many other lullabies began as a song that a mother sang to a child, and then was passed on through generations. Do you have a favorite lullaby?

A melody is a series of musical notes, played from left to right in a line, that makes a musical tune. You read a melody line just like you read a sentence. Melody is also one of the three fundamentals of music: melody, harmony, and rhythm. Can you think of a famous song you remember? If you can, it's because you remember the melody.

Meter is the way the beats of music are grouped together. Common time, or 4/4 time, means that there are four beats to every one measure. When you see this sign: $\frac{4}{4}$ or this sign: $\mathbf{C}$, four beats to a measure means a quarter note gets one beat. How many beats would a half note get?

M
m

The letter **M** is Melody.
A tune is what we hear
when music notes are played in line
and flow into our ear.

Yankee Doodle went to town, a riding on a po-ny, stuck a feather in his cap, and

And M is also Meter.
You can be a music star
when you learn the basic pace
is four beats in a bar.

One, two, three, and four!

mac-a-roni.

Yan-kee Doo-dle

Now **N** is for Note.
Can you follow along
with the notes on the staff
of your favorite song?

Each note fills a space
or sits right on a line.
The spaces spell FACE.
The lines spell
Every Good Boy Does Fine.

When you learn to read music, you learn that notes are labeled with letters of the alphabet. When you put them together to read, you can play musical sounds, just like reading words. Each note rests on a group of five lines and four spaces called a staff. There are two main clef signs, a G or treble clef, which looks like this: 𝄞 and a F or bass clef, which looks like this: 𝄢. In the treble clef, the spaces spell FACE and the lines spell out Every Good Boy Does Fine. In the bass clef, the lines spell Good Boys Do Fine Always, and the spaces spell All Cows Eat Grass.

And **O** is for the Orchestra
where people play as one.
Woodwinds, strings, percussion, brass—
it sounds like so much fun!

Encore, encore, please play one more!

O o

An orchestra is a mixed body of instrumentalists who work together performing symphonic music and other works. But there are several types of orchestras. A symphony orchestra is a group of usually 85 or more players who can play elaborate works of music, while a chamber orchestra is a small version of a symphony orchestra, usually consisting of 15 to 45 people. A string orchestra means that there are string instruments only, while a theater orchestra is a small group that plays to accompany theatrical productions.

P is for Percussion.
Come and move your feet.
It makes you feel like dancing when
percussion gives the beat!

Kettledrums are timpani,
bells and cymbals grand.
Find yourself some pots and pans
and make a kitchen band.

There are two types of percussion instruments: rhythmic, which means it plays a rhythm but no melody and includes all sorts of drums as well as timpani and cymbals; and melodic, which means the instrument can provide rhythm and melody, such as a xylophone. The percussion instruments provide rhythm and beat to music, and percussion players often get to play more than one type of percussion instrument.

Have you ever heard of a kitchen band? You can find all sorts of percussion instruments around your house. Cardboard boxes, plastic bowls, and pails are fun to drum. You can also fill plastic jugs and bottles with rice or beans to have an instrument to shake. Sound like fun? Give it a try!

Pp

There are many ways for people to organize their voices or instruments. One of the most common ways is with a quartet, which means four players or four singers. One such quartet is called the barbershop quartet, which is a type of music sung unaccompanied in four-part harmonies and rich chords. A duet means two people play or sing together, and is a popular way to share music with a friend. Have you heard of the tune called "Chopsticks"? It is a popular piano duet you may already know!

The letter Q is for Quartet—
    it means the number four.
Four singers or four players,
    it's a form we all adore.

Duet means two, quintet means five,
    a trio means there are three.
    Solo means all by yourself.
    It's easy as can be!

Q q

R r

R is for Rhythm.
Can you feel the beat
as it flows through our fingers
and into our feet?

And R is for Ragtime,
a hit for our nation.
Just drag out a beat
and it's called syncopation.

Rhythm is the beat we hear and feel. It is one of the three most important elements of music. There are many different types of rhythm: Some are very simple, while others can be very complex.

Ragtime is a type of music with a unique rhythm. It uses syncopation, which means the accents fall (drag out) at unexpected beats in the melody, while the bass line remains steady. In ragtime music, the melodic line will fall either on or off the beat, resulting in a lively and original sound. One of the most well-known musicians and composers of ragtime was Scott Joplin, born in the 1860s, who composed "The Maple Leaf Rag" and "The Entertainer."

S is for Strings.
They can play fast or slow.
Just pluck at them neatly
or draw with your bow.

The string family consists of many instruments including acoustic guitars, bass guitar, electric guitar, violin, cello, bass, viola, harp, lute, and zither. They are called strings because each instrument has some type of string stretched over them.

You make musical sounds when you pluck, bow, or strum the strings, which are made from gut, nylon, or wire. The strings are a beautiful part of any musical performance.

S s

T t

And T is for Tempo,
it's the pace we must go.
Allegro means fast
and lento means slow.

LARGO

Tempo is the speed of the music. The tempo is typically set by the conductor, or by written instructions on the sheet music.

The directions are usually given in Italian: Lento means to play slowly, while allegro means to play fast. There are many words to describe every tempo from the slowest to the fastest. These are fun words to learn. Presto is very fast and largo is the slowest.

The word unison means all together at the same pitch. Many times you will see this word printed at the beginning of a song. This means that everyone sings or plays the same part or melody together. When two or more instruments are playing in unison, it means they are playing the same notes.

U is for Unison—
"at the same time."
Let's all sing together,
and it will sound fine.

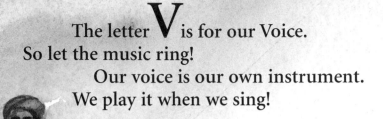

The letter **V** is for our Voice.
So let the music ring!
    Our voice is our own instrument.
We play it when we sing!

V

Our voice is the original instrument, because we make music when we hum or sing, and we can take it with us wherever we go! A song is a melody with words that has a beginning, middle, and an end, and it is what we sing. There are many types of voices in music, and they have names. To sing soprano means to sing the high notes, and to sing bass means to sing the lowest range of notes. An opera is a musical play where the actors sing all of the words.

V is also for virtuoso, which is someone who has exceptional musical talent and ability, either naturally inherited, earned through hard work and practice, or most often, a combination of both. Would you like to be a virtuoso?

The woodwind family includes the piccolo, flute, oboe, clarinet, English horn, saxophone, and bassoon. Woodwinds make music when air flows through a hollow tube and the player presses down on different keys, or holes, of the instrument.

Woodwind instruments were originally made from wood, but today some members, such as the flute, are made of metal or other materials. The bassoon, English horn, oboe, clarinet, and saxophone are reed instruments, which means they have a thin piece of plant fiber called a reed attached to the mouthpiece where the player blows. The saxophone is made of brass, but is derived from a wooden clarinet and is a favorite woodwind instrument.

Now **W** is for the Woodwinds—
they are shaped like hollow poles.
When the air flows through the tube,
it comes out through the holes.

Toot! Toot!

Bassoon

English Horn

The Woodwinds are a family,
and we must not forget
piccolo, flute, oboe, bassoon,
English horn, and clarinet.

Clarinet

flute

Piccolo

Xylophone begins with **X**.
I'm sure you understand
that all you need to play it is
a mallet in your hand.

Up and down the scale I go.
A little fast, a little slow.

X
X
X

The xylophone is a melodic percussion instrument. You can make a musical sound by striking it with a soft mallet. The xylophone has one or two rows of bars, similar to piano keys.

It is believed the xylophone originated in Southeast Asia, and was possibly brought to Africa during years of trade or migration. Slaves from Africa were taken to Latin America, bringing the xylophone with them, and from there, it was brought to the United States. This is one of the first instruments many children learn to play.

Yodel- ay- hee - hoooo

Now **Y** is for Yodel.
We sing without words
and make high and low noises.
It's neat—have you heard?

To yodel is to sing a song without words by alternating sounds from deep in your chest to high in your throat. Yodeling began in the Austrian Alps as a way for people to communicate from one mountain peak to another. Originally called Juchizn, each yell had a different meaning. Today, yodeling is an art form and an important part of European folk music.

Yy

Since ancient times, the zither has been one of the most widely used folk instruments because it was easy to make and play. It is a flat instrument with 30 to 40 strings over it and is played by strumming or plucking. Considered a folk instrument that evolved in the 18th century, the term zither is also applied to other similar instruments including the dulcimer and psaltery.

Long ago, most people were able to make their own zither out of wood and strings. Today, you can make a zither by placing rubber bands around an empty shoebox. Give it a good strum or pluck and see what sounds you can make!

And Z is for Zither,
a flat box with strings.
You strum them or pluck them.
You do many things.

Zz

Now here's the end
of our musical spree.
So please share your music
with love,
A to Z.

Q & A The Musical Way

1. What type of music helps soothe us into sleep?

2. What is the United States' national anthem? Canada's?

3. What instruments have tubing and a bell?

4. What instrument can we take with us wherever we go?

5. What type of music means it's the "music of people"?

6. What is the word for the pace the music goes?

7. How many singers or players are in a quartet?

8. What sound do we hear when two or more notes are played at the same time?

9. What is somebody called who writes music?

10. What are three types of early music?

Answers

1. Lullaby

2. "The Star Spangled Banner" and "O Canada"

3. The brass instruments

4. Our voice

5. Folk music

6. Tempo

7. Four

8. Harmony

9. A composer

10. Medieval, Renaissance, and Baroque

Kathy-jo Wargin

Children's author Kathy-jo Wargin began her writing career amidst the halls of the Music Department at the University of Minnesota-Duluth. Majoring in Music Theory and Composition, it was her love for combining rhythm and words that led her to pursue the field of writing for children. As the author of more than 17 books including the children's classic *The Legend of Sleeping Bear* and *The Edmund Fitzgerald: Song of the Bell*, she still enjoys making music with words. Kathy-jo lives in Petoskey, Michigan, with her husband, Ed, and son, Jake.

Katherine Larson

Award-winning artist Katherine Larson sold her first painting when she was 14 years old. She has made her living as an artist in every field from animated graphics and commercial art to commissioned paintings and murals across the United States. In addition to being a visual artist, Katherine is also an accomplished vocalist. She has won many national and international awards and has performed with many orchestras and opera companies starring in roles in *Madame Butterfly* and *Tosca*. She has trained in Italy and Germany and continues to do occasional vocal performances and often incorporates music and singing in her school presentations. *Melody* is her third book with Sleeping Bear Press. She also illustrated *G is for Grand Canyon: An Arizona Alphabet* and *A is for Arches: A Utah Alphabet*. Katherine lives in Ann Arbor, Michigan. Her website is www.katherinelarson.com.